3x (6/07)12/10

D0576992

Juneteenth

A Day to Celebrate Freedom From Slavery

Angela Leeper

3 1336 06924 5778

Enslow Publishers, Inc.

40 Industrial Road	PO Box 38
Box 398	Aldershot
Berkeley Heights, NJ 07922	Hants GU12 6BP
USA	UK

http://www.enslow.com

To my husband Brad, for all of his love and support

Library of Congress Cataloging-in-Publication Data

Leeper, Angela.
  Juneteenth : a day to celebrate freedom from slavery / Angela Leeper.
    v. cm.
    Includes bibliographical references and index.
    Contents: What is Juneteenth?—Early African-American history—Early Juneteenth celebrations—Juneteenth becomes a holiday—Juneteenth today.
    ISBN 0-7660-2206-4 (hardcover)
    1. Juneteenth—Juvenile literature. 2. Slaves—Emancipation—Texas—Juvenile literature. 3. African Americans—Texas—Galveston—History—Juvenile literature. 4. African Americans—Anniversaries, etc.—Juvenile literature. 5. African Americans—Social life and customs—Juvenile literature. 6. Slaves—Emancipation—United States—Juvenile literature.
[1. Juneteenth. 2. Slavery. 3. Holidays.] I. Title.
    E185.93.T4L44 2003
    394.263—dc21

                                                                                        2003008815

Printed in the United States of America

10 9 8 7 6 5 4 3 2 1

To Our Readers:
We have done our best to make sure that all Internet Addresses in this book were active and appropriate when we went to press. However, the author and publisher have no control over and assume no liability for the material available on those Internet sites or on other Web sites they may link to. Any comments or suggestions can be sent by e-mail to comments@enslow.com or to the address on the back cover.

Illustrations Credits: © Artville, LLC., pp. 8, 10; © Clipart.com, pp. 5, 7, 11, 18, 19, 22, 24, 26, © Corel Corporation, pp. 21, 39; © Kevin Berry, pp. i, ii, 3, 4, 6, 9, 30, 32, 37, 38, 40, 44, 45, 46, 47, 48; Associated Press, AP, Photographer Kelly West, Staff, p. 28; Associated Press, Photographer Bill Kidder, p. 25; Associated Press, ST. CLOUD TIMES, Photographer Joaquin Siopack, Member, p. 36; Associated Press, THE FACTS, Photographer Eric Lyle Kayne, p. 5; Associated Press, The Galveston County Daily News, Photographer Kevin Bartram, Member, p. 29; Cheryl Wells, pp. 42, 43; Enslow Publishers, Inc., pp. 16, 27, Library of Congress, pp. 12, 13, 14, 15, 17, 20, 31, 33, 34 Reproduced from the Dictionary of American Portraits, published by Dover Publications, Inc., in 1967, p. 12.

Cover Photos: Associated Press, The Facts, Photographer Eric Lyle Kayne, Inset-top; ©Kevin Berry, Background, Inset-bottom; Library of Congress, Inset-middle.

CONTENTS

Parades are an important part of a Juneteenth celebration.

CHAPTER 1
What Is Juneteenth?

Slaves in Texas learned that they were free on June 19, 1865. African Americans wanted to remember this day. So they made up a new word. They took the words "June" and "nineteenth" and combined them to make Juneteenth.

Cowboys and cowgirls ride horses down the street. Marching bands play music. Floats with many colors drive by. An African-American family claps and watches the parade.

After the parade, they go home. More family members come over. There is a barbecue in the backyard. Ribs cook over a fire. Homemade ice cream is good on this hot day. Everyone drinks red soda pop.

Some family members play baseball. Others tell stories from the past. At night,

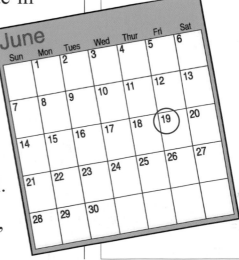

On Juneteenth, floats are part of the parade. Here, people get a float ready for the start of the parade.

fireworks light the sky. Everyone thinks about freedom.

This is not the Fourth of July (Independence Day). This is a special holiday for African Americans. On this day, they celebrate their freedom from slavery.

When the United States was new, many African Americans were slaves. They belonged to white slave owners. Slaves were property,

Slaves had to work many hours a day doing backbreaking labor, such as picking cotton.

like land or a house. They could be separated from their families at any time.

Slaves had a hard life. They worked long hours. They could not go to school. Slave owners could sell their slaves. Some slave owners were very cruel.

In Texas, all slaves found out they were free on June 19, 1865. This day is known as

Texas is the second largest state in the United States.

Juneteenth. At first, it was a holiday in Texas. Today, people celebrate Juneteenth all across the United States.

On Juneteenth, African Americans remember their ancestors. Ancestors are the people who lived before us. On this day, many African Americans also think about the future. They want all African Americans to have a good life. African Americans think about their own lives, too. They think of ways to be good people.

We all need to remember Juneteenth. A sad time in history ended. But every June 19, all Americans can celebrate freedom.

African Americans remember their African ancestors with artwork. Artwork like this can be seen during Juneteenth.

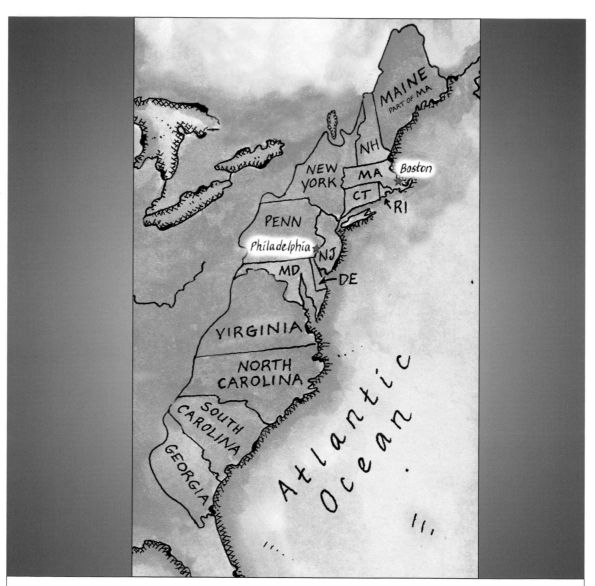

The thirteen colonies as they looked before the Revolutionary War. Philadelphia and Boston were important cities during the war.

CHAPTER 2

Early African-American History

★

Plantations are large farms that raise crops such as tobacco or cotton. Plantations in the South before the Civil War usually had a "Great House," like the one shown here, where the owners lived.

The first Africans arrived in America at Jamestown, Virginia, in 1619. At this time, Virginia was a colony that belonged to England. Virginia was mostly made up of farms and plantations, or large estates that produced great quantities of crops. These first African men and women worked as indentured servants to pay for their passage to America. But as time went on, Africans

Slaves were brought from Africa to America, where they were traded for food or sold as plantation workers.

who arrived in America were made to work as slaves.

As more colonies were formed, plantation owners needed more slaves for labor. Millions of African slaves were brought to America between the 1680s and 1865. Many worked on plantations that raised tobacco, rice, and cotton.

The colonies wanted to become their own country. On July 4, 1776, the colonists

The colonists fought many battles against Great Britain to win their independence.

Slavery was one of the reasons for the Civil War.

declared their freedom and fought against Great Britain in the Revolutionary War. The colonies won their freedom and became known as the United States of America.

Today, the United States celebrates this freedom, or independence, on July 4, which is called Independence Day. But not all Americans became free on July 4, 1776. African Americans remained slaves.

After the Revolutionary War ended, most slave owners lived in the southern part of the United States. Many people in the North were against slavery. The North and South could not agree on many issues. One of the biggest issues was slavery.

Black soldiers fought and died bravely in the Civil War.

As a result, eleven states in the South seceded, or left, the United States in 1860 and 1861. The Confederate states breaking away from the Union began the American Civil War.

Abraham Lincoln was president during the Civil War. He did not believe that people should be slaves. On January 1, 1863, he issued the Emancipation Proclamation, a

This map shows what states made up the Confederacy and what states made up the Union.

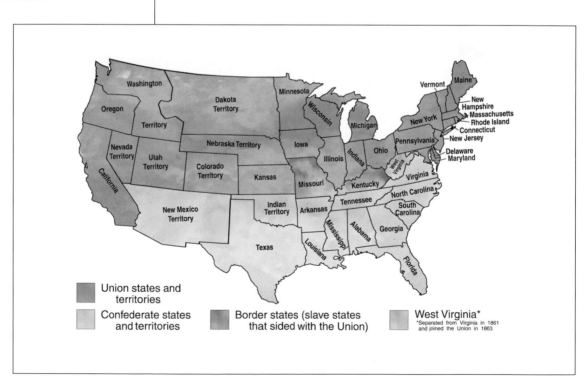

Abraham Lincoln is known as the Great Emancipator because he worked hard to end slavery.

document that granted slaves in every state their freedom. But because the country was at war, the South did not obey this proclamation.

The Civil War ended on April 9, 1865, when the South surrendered to the North. All slaves in the Confederate states were finally

Confederate general Robert E. Lee (right) surrendered to Union general Ulysses S. Grant (left) at Appomattox Court House in Virginia.

supposed to be free. But because there were no telephones, television, or the Internet, the news of emancipation spread slowly. Some people did not find out about the end of the war until weeks or months later.

Some slave owners did not tell their slaves about the end of the war. These African Americans did not know that they had been freed. The army was sent into the South to make sure that African-American people understood their new freedom.

Major General Gordon Granger read General Order Number 3 to the citizens of Galveston, Texas.

The people of Texas are informed that in accordance with the Proclamation from the Executive of the United States, all slaves are free . . .

General Gordon Granger Galveston 1865

Texas was the farthest state that had seceded from the Union. African Americans there were some of the last people to hear about the Emancipation Proclamation and the end of the Civil War.

On June 19, 1865, Major General Gordon Granger read a document called General Order Number 3 to the citizens of Galveston, Texas. This order explained that according to the Emancipation Proclamation, slaves in Texas were free. This was over one year after the end of the

Civil War. It was almost two and a half years after the Emancipation Proclamation had been issued.

The Constitution is the chief set of laws of the United States. Amendments, or changes, have been added to the Constitution to update the laws. The Thirteenth Amendment to the Constitution was ratified, or approved, in 1865. This amendment officially ended all slavery in the United States.

Today, African Americans remember the end of slavery with the Juneteenth holiday. It is celebrated every June 19, the same day African Americans heard about their freedom in Galveston, Texas, in 1865.

Under the word "Emancipation," African Americans can be seen enjoying a comfortable home life. The left side of the picture shows scenes of the past, including the selling of slaves. The right side of the picture shows scenes of the future, including education and fair employment.

CHAPTER 3

Early Juneteenth Celebrations

O ne year after Major General Granger read General Order Number 3, the first Juneteenth holiday was celebrated in Texas. Early celebrations began with parades. Bands played music. Horses pulled floats.

Former slaves marched proudly in their towns. Compared to their owners, slaves had worn ragged clothing. During slavery, there were even laws against African Americans dressing up. The slaves were also required to

EMANCIPATION PARKS

African Americans wanted to celebrate Juneteenth in a special place. In Texas, they raised money and bought land to be used as parks. One of these parks is Booker T. Washington Park, named for the famous black educator. It is in Mexia, Texas. Today, many cities have Juneteenth or Emancipation parks.

Many African Americans gave thanks upon hearing about being freed from slavery.

move out of the way to let white people pass. Now, African Americans were free to dress up in new clothes and march in the streets.

Juneteenth was a serious time. The Emancipation Proclamation and General Order Number 3 were read. Former slaves told stories about their lives and how they fought against slavery. Religious leaders, educators, and former slaves gave moving speeches. They encouraged African-American people to live and work honestly. African Americans went to church services to give thanks to God for their new freedom.

Juneteenth was also a time for fun. Family members gathered for picnics and family reunions. Lamb, pork, and beef were cooked in barbecue pits. These were special meats. Not everyone could afford these foods every day. Other special foods included red soda pop and homemade cake and ice cream.

There were many ways to celebrate. Some African Americans listened to music and attended dances. Others went fishing. The most popular activities were playing baseball and watching cowboys in rodeos.

All these traditions started in Texas. Some African Americans left Texas and moved to other states, such as Oklahoma, Arkansas, Louisiana, California, and Florida. They took these traditions with them and celebrated Juneteenth in their new locations.

Even today, many Juneteenth celebrations feature rodeos.

Street fairs are often held during Juneteenth. Many crafts with African designs can be seen.

CHAPTER 4

Juneteenth Becomes a Holiday

Juneteenth has been celebrated in Texas every year since 1865. It is the oldest African-American holiday. Representative Al Edwards from Houston, Texas, wanted to make Juneteenth a legal state holiday in Texas. On legal holidays, like the Fourth of July and Thanksgiving, people do not work. Government offices, schools, banks, and post offices are closed. This gives people more time to be with their families to celebrate the holiday.

Representative Edwards introduced a bill in

Representative Al Edwards worked hard to make Juneteenth a state holiday in Texas.

the Texas legislature, where state laws are decided. The bill would make Juneteenth a legal state holiday. It was passed on June 7, 1979, and became a law. Juneteenth was celebrated as a legal state holiday for the first time on June 19, 1980.

Other states now honor Juneteenth as a holiday. These states include Delaware, Oklahoma, Georgia, Florida, Idaho, Iowa, Vermont, Alaska, Washington, Maryland, Kentucky, and Louisiana. In some states, Juneteenth is a legal holiday. In other states, it is an observed holiday, like Flag Day, Mother's Day, and Father's Day. Many other states have introduced bills that would make Juneteenth a state holiday. Some organizations are trying to make Juneteenth a national holiday so that all Americans can honor the day. In 1997, the United States Congress proclaimed June 19 "Juneteenth Independence Day."

Many Juneteenth celebrations take place in the United States. The celebrations are held in Milwaukee, Wisconsin; Minneapolis, Minnesota; Chicago, Illinois; Berkeley, California; Atlanta, Georgia; and Richmond, Virginia. Other major cities hold Juneteenth celebrations, too. But some of the biggest celebrations are still in Texas, in the cities of Houston, Dallas, Austin, Fort Worth, and San Antonio.

Each year in Texas, an Emancipation Trail Ride is held. Riders celebrate Juneteenth by traveling one mile for every year since the Emancipation Proclamation was read aloud in Galveston.

African Americans march with pride in Juneteenth parades.

CHAPTER 5

Juneteenth Today

START YOUR OWN JUNETEENTH

★

If there are no Juneteenth celebrations where you live, you can start your own. Invite your family and friends. Read the Emancipation Proclamation and General Order Number 3. Have a picnic. Sing songs. Tell family stories.

Today, Juneteenth is celebrated much like it was when the holiday first began. Instead of one day, though, it may be celebrated for a week. Some cities have Juneteenth activities during the entire month of June.

African-American families still get together for Juneteenth. They watch parades like their ancestors did. Bands are still a part of the parades. Cowboys ride on their horses. African-American members of community groups and the military march, ride horses, or ride on floats.

This float was part of a Juneteenth parade in San Francisco.

Floats are now pulled by cars. One float may carry Miss Juneteenth.

The Emancipation Proclamation and General Order Number 3 are still read out loud today. Religious leaders, community leaders, and educators still give speeches and tell stories about the fight to end slavery. They talk about abolitionists like Harriet Tubman and Frederick Douglass. These people believed

Harriet Tubman became known for her daring rescues that helped slaves escape to freedom.

Frederick Douglass devoted his life to fighting for the rights of African Americans.

that slavery was wrong. They helped to end slavery.

They also talk about civil rights leaders, such as Reverend Dr. Martin Luther King, Jr., and Rosa Parks. These leaders helped African-American people in the 1950s and 1960s.

Reverend Dr. Martin Luther King, Jr., was one of the most important civil rights leaders of all time.

They wanted African Americans to have the same rights as white people. Some of these rights were going to school and voting. Both abolitionists and civil rights leaders risked their lives to help African Americans. On Juneteenth, many of these brave African-American people are remembered.

Many other Juneteenth traditions continue today. African Americans still go to religious

This family sang together at a Texas Juneteenth celebration.

Barbecues have been part of Juneteenth celebrations from the beginning. This barbecue was at Riverside Park in St. Cloud, Minnesota.

services and picnics. They tell family stories. They participate in baseball games, foot races, rodeos, and dances. Red soda pop, barbecue, and other foods from early Juneteenth celebrations are still popular today. Some African Americans celebrate with new clothes. Fireworks now end the long day.

Music has also become a large part of

Music of all kinds can be heard at Juneteenth celebrations.

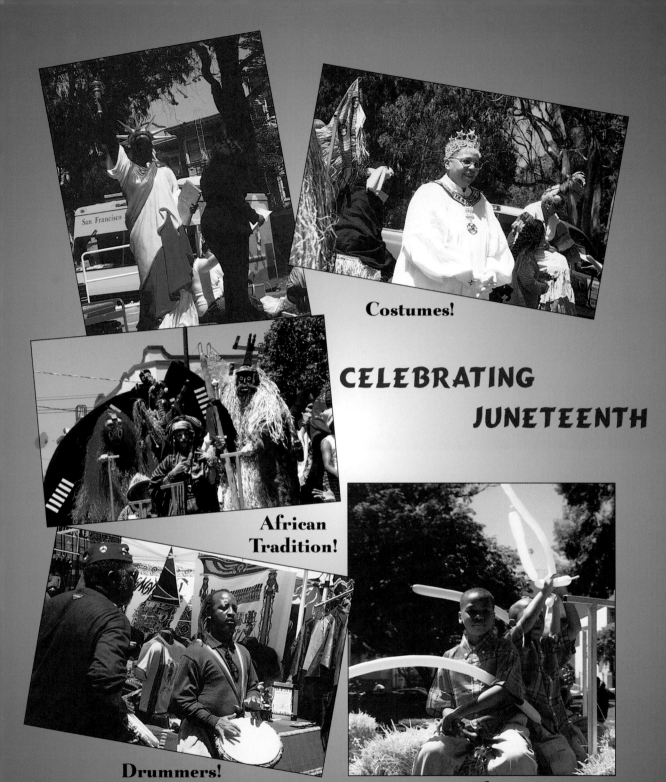

Costumes!

CELEBRATING JUNETEENTH

African Tradition!

Drummers!

Floats!

38

Juneteenth. There are many gospel and jazz concerts on or around Juneteenth.

Today, there is even a national celebration in the nation's capital, Washington, D.C. It is called Washington Juneteenth. This Juneteenth celebration is like many others around the country. It includes religious services, speeches, and music concerts.

The U.S. Capitol Building is in Washington, D.C. The Juneteenth celebration in Washington, D.C. is called Washington Juneteenth.

Juneteenth is a time for African Americans to remember the past and celebrate the present.

Juneteenth remains an important holiday for African Americans. It is still a time for thinking. African Americans continue to remember the horrible time of slavery and the brave men and women who fought to end it. Juneteenth also still means looking to the future. African Americans continue to help each other become better people.

Juneteenth is a time all Americans need to remember. We can all celebrate the end of slavery. We can respect each other and be glad that all Americans are free today!

This young man plays a drum that was once used by slaves. It was one of the many instruments on display as part of a Juneteenth celebration in Natchez, Mississippi.

Juneteenth Project

★

Juneteenth Flag Pinwheels

Decorate for Juneteenth. Make some pinwheels to place in your garden, yard, or in your window!

You will need:

✔ **construction paper**

✔ **scissors**

✔ **markers or crayons**

✔ **push-pin or thumbtack**

✔ **pencil with an eraser or craft stick**

1. Cut two squares of the same size from construction paper.

2. Fold the corner of each square over into a triangle.

3. Fold each triangle in half. Unfold the paper.

4. Using crayons or markers, decorate one side of each square with the Juneteenth flag.

5. Put the undecorated sides of each square together. Cut along each of the four fold lines, about halfway to the middle of the square.

6. Still holding both squares together, punch four holes—one in each corner.

7. Gently gather each of the four points to the center. Be careful not to crease the paper.

8. Push a push-pin or thumbtack through the center to attach the pinwheel to the side of a pencil's eraser, or into a craft stick.

9. Blow gently on your Juneteenth pinwheel to watch it spin!

Words to Know
★

abolitionists—Individuals who believed that slavery was wrong and helped to end it.

ancestor—A person from whom one is descended.

civil rights—Basic human rights, like voting and going to school, which are guaranteed by law to all people.

Civil War—The war fought in the United States between the North and South from 1861 to 1865. One of the main causes was slavery.

emancipation—Freedom from slavery.

Words to Know

★

Emancipation Proclamation—President Abraham Lincoln's order on January 1, 1863, to free all slaves in the United States.

General Order Number 3—An announcement read aloud in Galveston, Texas, on June 19, 1865, which told slaves that they were free.

indentured servants—People who agree to work for a certain period of time to pay off a debt, such as the cost of coming to another country.

secede—When part of a country separates from the rest of the country.

tradition—The practice of passing down customs, beliefs, or other knowledge from parents to children.

Reading About

Branch, Muriel Miller. *Juneteenth: Freedom Day*. New York: Dutton, 1998.

Jordan, Denise M., *Juneteenth Day*. Chicago: Heinemann Library, 1998.

Levy, Janey. *Juneteenth: Celebrating the End of Slavery*. New York: Rosen, 2003.

Olson, Kay Melchisedech, *Africans in American, 1619–1865*. Mankato, Minn.: Blue Earth Books, 2003.

Warner, Penny, *Kids' Holiday Fun: Great Family Activities Every Month of the Year*. Minnetonka, Minn: Meadowbrook Press, 1994.

Winchester, Faith. *African American Holidays*. Mankato, Minn.: Bridgestone Books, 1996.

Internet Addresses

★

THE HANDBOOK OF TEXAS ONLINE: JUNETEENTH
http://www.tsha.utexas.edu/handbook/online/
   articles/view/JJ/lkjl.html

JUNETEENTH.COM
http://www.juneteenth.com
Find out more about the history of Juneteenth.

SOCIAL STUDIES FOR KIDS
THE IMPORTANCE OF JUNETEENTH
http://www.socialstudiesforkids.com/articles/
   holidays/juneteenth.htm

Index

★